Coral Reefs

Kristie Pickersgill

Illustrated by Sara Ugolotti

Additional illustrations by Gal Weizman

Designed by Sam Whibley, Claire Morgan and Jenny Hastings

Coral reef consultant: Professor Steve Simpson,
Marine Biology and Global Change, University of Bristol

Reading consultant: Alison Kelly

Contents

Busy reefs

Coral reefs are found in warm, shallow seas all over the world.

They are home to lots of fish, other sea animals and plants.

What is coral?

Corals are living things that look like amazing rocks or plants. They can be hard or soft.

This hard coral looks like a human brain.

Soft corals bend and sway in the water.

Each coral is made up of lots of small animals called polyps.

Polyp

Algae

Very tiny plants called algae live inside the polyps.

The algae turn sunlight into food. This helps the coral to grow.

Reef builders

Coral reefs are made by hard corals.
It takes a long time for them to grow.

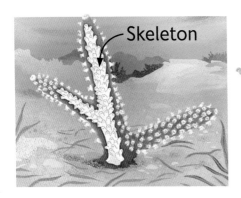

Inside every hard coral, the polyps build a skeleton.

The coral gets bigger as the polyps add to the skeleton.

If the coral grows close to other corals, they form a reef.

Later, more corals grow on the reef, so it gets even bigger.

The Great Barrier Reef in Australia has been growing for thousands of years.

It's made up of almost 3,000 coral reefs.

Who lives on reefs?

Thousands of different types of creatures live on a coral reef.

There are bright tropical fish that swim in big groups.

Crabs, sea snails and starfish crawl slowly over the reef.

Rays and sharks glide
above looking for
things to eat.

Octopuses and eels
squeeze into holes
and cracks to hide.

Stinging tentacles

Sea creatures called anemones cling to coral reefs.

Tentacle

Mouth

An anemone has long, thin parts called tentacles. They stick out around its mouth.

The anemone uses its tentacles to sting fish that swim by.

Then the anemone pulls the fish into its mouth to eat.

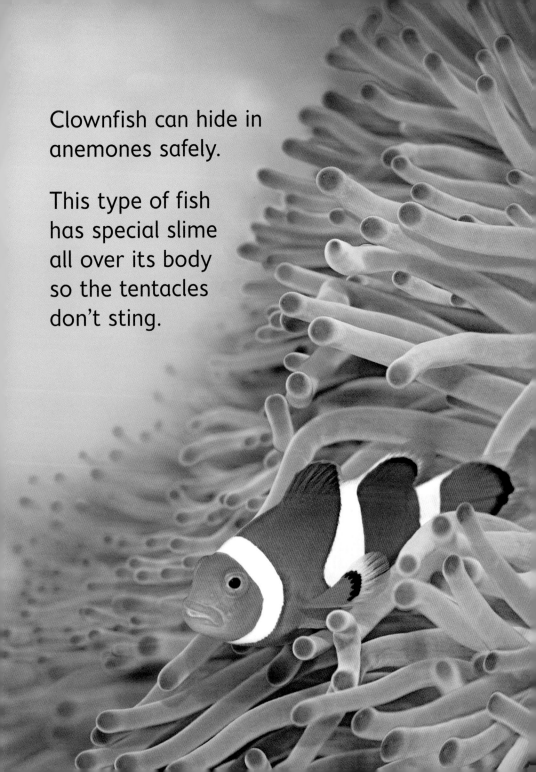

Clownfish can hide in anemones safely.

This type of fish has special slime all over its body so the tentacles don't sting.

Coral crunchers

Parrotfish live on most reefs. They crunch coral to eat the algae growing on it.

This stoplight parrotfish is using its strong teeth to bite some coral.

At night, parrotfish
find gaps in the reef
where they rest.

Before sleeping,
each fish makes
a bubble of spit
around its body.

The bubble keeps out
bugs. It also traps the
fish's smell inside, so
sharks can't find it.

All the pieces of coral that parrotfish
swallow pass out as sand.

Creature cleaners

Fish and turtles sometimes visit part of a reef where smaller animals clean them.

A porcupine fish swims up to a table coral and waits.

Soon little fish called cleaner wrasse dart out from the coral.

Then the wrasse nibble bugs off the porcupine fish's skin.

These hungry fish are cleaning a
green sea turtle.

They're eating
algae that grow
on its shell and
slow it down.

Reef sounds

Creatures on coral reefs make lots of different sounds. Tiny snapping shrimp are the loudest.

A snapping shrimp opens its big claw when a crab crawls by.

Then it snaps the claw shut. This makes a bubble shoot out.

The bubble bursts with a loud pop stunning the crab.

Now the crab can't move, so the shrimp can eat it.

Male damselfish purr and dance to attract females.

These fish are called sweetlips. They make grunting noises when they're scared.

Blending in

Many animals use the way they look to hide on coral reefs.

Here a seahorse has bumpy skin which matches the coral it clings to with its tail.

If an octopus spots a monk seal, it dives down to the reef.

Then the octopus makes its skin lighter so that it blends in.

There's a frogfish hunting on this reef. Can you spot its mouth and one of its eyes?

Super sponges

Animals called sponges grow on coral reefs.
They help to keep the water clear.

This is a tube sponge. It sucks dirt and tiny
living things through its sides and eats them.

Then it
pumps out
clean water
at the top.

If sponges get too big, they can stop sunlight from reaching the reef.

But hawksbill turtles eat big sponges. They break off chunks with their mouths.

As they eat more and more chunks, the turtles let the sunlight through.

Baby corals

Every year, corals release millions of eggs.

Each polyp in this staghorn coral is
squeezing out a tiny ball full of eggs.

Corals always release their eggs at night.

First, the eggs float up to the surface from the reef.

Then each egg drifts through the ocean and slowly changes shape.

When it settles on the ocean floor, it grows into a baby coral.

All kinds of reefs

Reefs grow in different shapes and sizes, and in different parts of the sea.

Many reefs form next to land. They're called fringing reefs.

Barrier reefs are
separated from land
by calm, deep water.

Atolls are incredible islands made of coral.
They're ring-shaped, like this one.

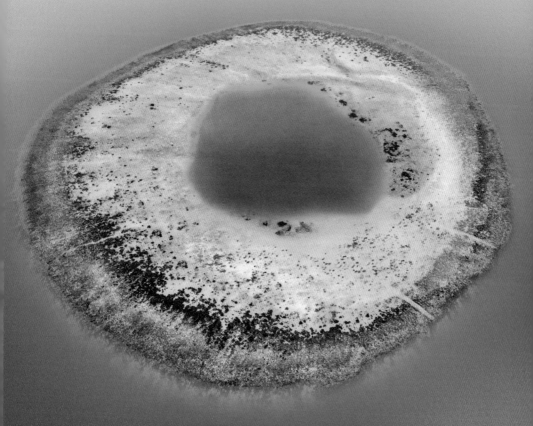

Deep reefs

There are coral reefs in cold, deep parts of the ocean too.

Down here, it's very dark. The corals can't get any food from sunlight.

They catch tiny animals called zooplankton to eat instead.

Deep reefs are hard to reach. Scientists use submarines to explore them.

Some deep-sea corals glow when fish bump into them.

Rescuing reefs

Across the world, seas are getting warmer.

Warmer water makes corals push out the algae that live inside them.

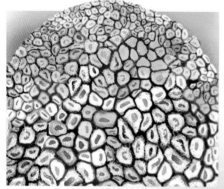

Without their algae, corals start to turn white. This is known as bleaching.

Bleached corals don't have enough food to grow. They'll die if the water stays too warm.

Bleached coral can recover if the sea cools down.

People are studying reefs to find out how they can save them.

This diver is measuring a bleached coral.

Glossary

Here are some of the words in this book you might not know. This page tells you what they mean.

 reef – a hard ridge under the sea. Coral reefs are built by hard corals.

 polyp – a small, squishy animal. Lots of polyps make up each coral.

 algae – tiny types of plants. They make food from sunlight.

 skeleton – the hard part inside some types of coral.

 tentacle – a long, thin body part. Some sea creatures have tentacles that sting.

 zooplankton – tiny animals that float in the sea. There are lots of different kinds.

 bleach – to turn white. Corals are bleached when the sea is too warm.

Usborne Quicklinks

Would you like to find out more about coral reefs, and the amazing creatures that live on them? Visit Usborne Quicklinks for links to websites with videos, facts and activities.

Go to **usborne.com/Quicklinks** and type in the keywords "**beginners coral reefs**". Make sure you ask a grown-up before going online.

Notes for grown-ups

Please read the internet safety guidelines at Usborne Quicklinks with your child. Children should be supervised online. The websites are regularly reviewed and the links at Usborne Quicklinks are updated. However, Usborne Publishing is not responsible and does not accept liability for the content or availability of any website other than its own.

The two orange creatures on this coral are called feather stars.

Index

Acknowledgements

Photographic manipulation by John Russell and Nick Wakeford

Photo credits

The publishers are grateful to the following for permission to reproduce material:
cover © Brandon Cole/naturepl.com; **p.1** © Alex Mustard/naturepl.com; **pp.2-3** © Alex Mustard/naturepl.com;
p.4 © Seaphotoart/Alamy Stock Photo; **p.7** © Inaki Relanzon/naturepl.com; **p.11** © Aflo/naturepl.com;
pp.12-13 © Stephen Frink/Stephen Frink Collection/Alamy Stock Photo; **p.15** © WaterFrame/Alamy Stock Photo;
pp.16-17 © Alex Mustard/naturepl.com; **p.18** © Tim Laman/naturepl.com; **p.19** © Alex Mustard/naturepl.com;
p.20 © John Anderson/Alamy Stock Photo; **p.22** © Juergen Freund/naturepl.com; **p.24** © Michael Nolan/robertharding;
p.25 © Mlenny/Getty Images; **p.27** © SeaTops/Alamy Stock Photo; **p.29** © Rainer von Brandis/Getty Images;
p.31 © Franco Banfi/naturepl.com.

Every effort has been made to trace and acknowledge ownership of copyright. If any rights have
been omitted, the publishers offer to rectify this in any subsequent editions following notification.

Sun, Moon and Stars

Farm Animals

Elizabeth I

Rubbish & Recycling

Dogs

Horses & Ponies

Cats

Ancient Greeks

Spiders

VOLCANOES

DINOSAURS

Your Body

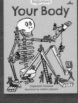

Armour

Sharks

The Celts

VIKINGS

Castles

How Flowers grow

Digging up the past

Caterpillars & Butterflies

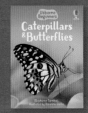

Ballet

Pirates

EGYPTIANS

Eggs & Chicks

ROMANS

Weather

Tadpoles & Frogs

Why do we eat?

Under the Sea

Bears

AZTECS

Usborne Beginners
Trucks

Usborne Beginners
Night Animals

Usborne Beginners
Firefighters

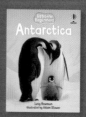
Usborne Beginners
Antarctica

Usborne Beginners
Bugs

COWBOYS

Usborne Beginners
PLANET EARTH

Usborne Beginners
London

Usborne Beginners
Seashore

Usborne Beginners
China

Usborne Beginners
Dangerous Animals

Usborne Beginners
Rainforests

Usborne Beginners
Trees

Usborne Beginners
Bats

Ships

Usborne Beginners
Reptiles

Usborne Beginners
Trains

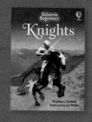
Usborne Beginners
Knights

Usborne Beginners
The Solar System

Monkeys

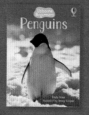
Penguins

Usborne Beginners
Elephants

Usborne Beginners
Tigers

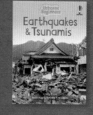
Usborne Beginners
Earthquakes & Tsunamis

Usborne Beginners
Storms and Hurricanes

Usborne Beginners
BEES & WASPS

Usborne Beginners
Wolves

Usborne Beginners
Owls

Usborne Beginners
Snakes